## DISCOVERING CANADA

# The Defenders

### ROBERT LIVESEY & A.G. SMITH

Stoddart

First published in 1994 by
Stoddart Publishing Co. Limited
34 Lesmill Road
Toronto, Canada
M3B 2T6
(416) 445-3333

CANADIAN CATALOGUING IN PUBLICATION DATA

Livesey, Robert, 1940-
   The defenders

(Discovering Canada)
ISBN 0-7737-5665-5

1. Canada - History - War of 1812 - Juvenile
literature. I. Smith, A.G. (Albert Gray),
1945-        . II. Title.   III. Series: Livesey,
Robert, 1940-        .   Discovering Canada.

FC442.L58 1994    j971.03′4    C94-931321-1
E359.85.L58 1994

TEXT ILLUSTRATIONS: A.G. Smith
COVER ILLUSTRATION: A.G. Smith
COVER DESIGN: Brant Cowie/ArtPlus Limited


Printed in Canada

*Stoddart Publishing gratefully acknowledges the support of the Canada Council, Ontario Ministry of Culture, Tourism, and Recreation, Ontario Arts Council, and Ontario Publishing Centre in the development of writing and publishing in Canada.*

*To Cousins Brett and Kara,*
*with love*


*A special thanks to Scott Baltjes, Ron Dale, Josie Hazen,*
*Vicky Kosharewich, Elsha Leventis, Warren Simpson, David Webb,*
*the librarians at the Oakville Public Library, the Sheridan College Library,*
*the University of Windsor Library, and all of the 1812 re-enactors*
*(from whom I have learned so much) for their help in producing this book.*

Other books in the Discovering Canada series

*The Vikings*

*The Fur Traders*

*New France*

*Native Peoples*

# Contents

# Introduction

Canadians are a peace-loving people. Unlike many nations, Canada came into existence without violence or revolution or bloodshed. We consider no country our enemy, and no countries have reason to hate us. Our closest neighbour is the United States of America and between our two nations is the longest undefended border in the world.

But Canadians are not weak or timid. If we are attacked, we are quick to defend ourselves. When our friends around the world have disputes with their neighbours, Canada is one of the first countries to go to their aid or volunteer to act as a peacekeeping force.

It was long ago, in the year 1812, that Canada was invaded by the United States, and we were forced to defend our borders and lives. At that time, Canada consisted of several colonies under British protection. When Britain became involved in a long war with France, the Americans, eager to expand their territory to include all of North America, thought that Canada could be easily conquered because the English would be too busy with the war in Europe to be able to defend their North American colonies. The former American president, Thomas Jefferson, boasted that the conquest of Canada was a "mere matter of marching."

The Canadians were outnumbered ten to one, and there were only 4000 British troops in the Canadas at the time. When President Madison of the United States declared war on June 18, 1812, there

1

were eight million Americans and only three hundred thousand Canadians. To make matters more complicated, more than half of the settlers in Upper Canada had arrived recently from the United States. America had a large, experienced army; Canada had only a small force of tough British professional soldiers, supported by native warriors and untrained volunteers from its farms and towns. It was to be one of the most uneven wars in history. The Canadians would have to use all their intelligence and imagination if they were to successfully defend themselves against such a powerful force.

## War Hawks

In addition to the desire to control all of North America, two main issues encouraged the United States to declare war on Britain. One

was the American expansion in the Northwest. The new settlers were in conflict with the native tribes who had always lived and hunted in those territories. Many Americans, known as "war hawks," believed that the Canadians, who traded furs peacefully with their native partners, were encouraging them to block the Yankee settlers.

One of the ambitious American leaders, General William Henry Harrison, attacked the native village of Prophet's Town on November 17, 1811, at what was to become known as the Battle of Tippecanoe. It was the home of two Shawnee brothers, The Prophet and Leaping Panther, who dreamed of a native confederacy that would occupy the land from Lake Erie in the north to as far south as Florida. Thousands of braves from a half dozen tribes had joined with the two Shawnee chiefs.

Harrison beat back the natives and burnt their village. He would later use his victory to be elected president of the United States.

## Friction on the High Seas

A second cause of trouble leading to the war was that the British had issued orders-in-council that permitted their navy to stop and search American ships at sea. The British wanted to prevent the United States from sending trade goods or supplies to France while they were at war. Also, Yankee shippers and the U.S. navy encouraged deserters from the British navy with higher pay and phony documents stating that they were Americans. The British would board American vessels at sea, search them, and force former British seamen to return to serve in the war; however, some American sailors were taken due to mistaken identity.

## An Unnecessary War?

Back in 1812, it took several weeks for news to travel by ship across the Atlantic Ocean. When the U.S. Congress declared war on June 18, 1812, it was a close vote. No one knew that one of the main complaints no longer existed; Britain had suspended its orders-in-council two days before.

A MARINE ON WATCH

5

# Weapons of the War

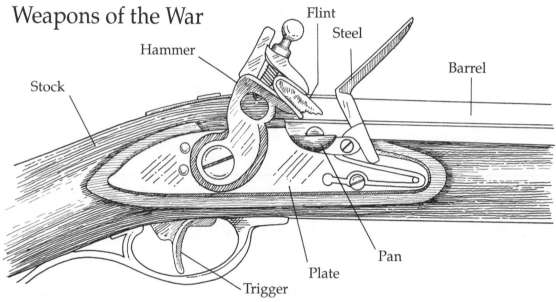

Stock · Hammer · Flint · Steel · Barrel · Trigger · Plate · Pan

*Brown Bess*

The flintlock musket issued to the British regular army during the War of 1812 was known as "Brown Bess," and it took 19 steps to fire it. It shot small four-gram balls but was not very accurate. The soldiers would aim their weapons in the direction of the enemy and, at the order of the officer in command, fire at the same time. The spray of bullets and the deafening blasts of the muskets along with the billows of blue smoke that were produced created a frenzied atmosphere. Despite the long, awkward weapon, a Canadian could reload and fire two or three times a minute. Many Americans carried their own weapons such as the Harpers Ferry rifle or the "Tennessee Rifle" (actually manufactured in Pennsylvania), which were far more accurate than the muskets but also slower to load.

## Bombs and Grasshoppers

The cannons used during the war were deadly and devastating. They were named by the weight of the pig iron balls called "round-shot" that they fired: three-pounders (1.4 kg), six-pounders (2.7 kg), nine-pounders (4 kg), twelve-pounders (5.4 kg), eighteen-pounders (8.2 kg), twenty-four-pounders (11 kg). Shells were stuffed with powder, creating "bombs" that would explode in mid-air, spraying dozens of deadly fragments over the enemy lines. The deadliest projectiles were grape shot and case shot. Some of the little three-pounders were also nicknamed "grasshoppers," because the carriages on which they were mounted would bounce, or "jump," when they were fired.

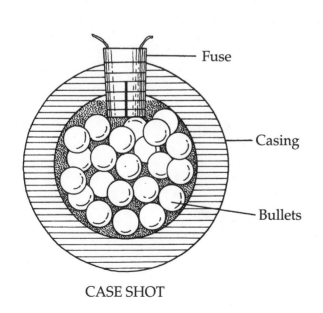

CASE SHOT

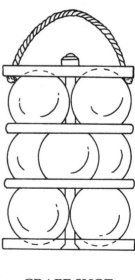

GRAPE SHOT

8

# CHAPTER 1

# *Hero of Upper Canada*

## *General Isaac Brock*

One man was mainly responsible for Canada's victory over the invading American armies in 1812. Isaac Brock stood two metres, had fair hair and blue eyes. He was a tough, bold, and daring professional soldier. Explaining how his small force defeated an overwhelming enemy, he once said, "I speak loud and look big."

Brock arrived in Canada from England in 1802, sailing up the St. Lawrence with the 49th British Regiment. The following year, he single-handedly suppressed a dangerous conspiracy, which had been instigated by deserters from a detachment at Fort George. He had complete knowledge of the French language as well as his native English and felt such a loyalty to the land and the people of Canada that he refused a post in Spain in order to remain here. By 1811, he was a major-general and had been appointed the provisional lieutenant-governor of Upper Canada.

On June 18, 1812, the United States declared war on Canada, and one of the most uneven wars in history began. The Americans had a dream that was to become known as "manifest destiny"; they wished to occupy all of North America. The U.S. plan was to invade with two armies: General Hull's army via Fort Detroit, and General Van Rensselaer's force at Niagara. They believed that they could conquer Upper Canada (Ontario) by the end of 1812 and

proceed to Lower Canada (Quebec) to capture Montreal by the summer of 1813.

On July 12, 1812, General Hull, with a threatening demand that Canada surrender, led an army of 2000 Americans into Upper Canada. But Isaac Brock had gone into action before him and ordered a July 16th attack against Fort Michilimackinac on Mackinac Island, which controlled the northwestern fur trade on the Huron-Michigan Strait.

The commander of the Canadian force on St. Joseph's Island was Captain Charles Roberts of the 10th Royal Veterans. He was aided by John Askin Jr., the leader of a mixture of fur traders, voyageurs, and militia, and Robert Dickson, a Scottish-born giant of two

10

metres whose long, bright-crimson hair earned him his Sioux name of Mascotopah, "The Flaming-Haired Man." Dickson lived as a chief with his native wife and hunted in the present-day states of Minnesota, Wisconsin, and Iowa. Their easy and bloodless victory (the U.S. commander was not aware that war had been declared) created confidence among the natives and fur traders of the Northwest. When Hull's advancing army retreated back to the safety of Fort Detroit, Brock advanced and met the famous Shawnee chief, Leaping Panther, who was eager to join the Canadians so he could free his native lands and reap revenge for the burning of his village at Tippecanoe. They decided to attack Fort Detroit immediately.

## Capture of Fort Detroit

General Hull was particularly frightened of the natives, so Brock brazenly bluffed his opponent with a demand for surrender. He sent a message to the American commander which read: "You must be aware that the numerous body of Indians who have attached themselves to my troops will be beyond control the moment the contest commences."

That night the natives silently crossed the river and grouped in the woods behind the fort, where they began to terrify the American troops with wild war whoops and signal calls. At dawn on August 16, 1812, Brock, in scarlet and gold uniform and mounted on his famous grey horse, Alfred, appeared in full view of the enemy. Leaping Panther rode at his side in colourful war regalia.

Brock had encouraged his scanty force of untrained militia men, rounded up from the farms and villages of Upper Canada, to march in extended order and wear red coats to create the impression of a large number of professional soldiers. Brock had only five big guns on the river opposite Detroit, yet the American fort contained 33 large cannons.

Brock's bluff worked. When the first shells began to drop inside the fort, Hull surrendered his 2500 soldiers to Brock's small force of less than 800 without a fight. The victory meant that the Canadians controlled most of the Michigan Territory.

13

# Battle of Queenston Heights

The U.S. general of the central army, Van Rensselaer, had 6300 men; Brock had only 1500. One month after the capture of Fort Detroit, on the dark, wet morning of October 13, 1812, the Americans struck. A force of about 1500 crossed the Niagara River at the Canadian village of Queenston, opposite Lewiston, New York.

During the battle, a young American officer, Captain Wool, scaled Queenston Heights and occupied it. Brock, realizing that whoever controlled the Heights would win the battle, gathered about 90 men for a counterattack and, in a plumed hat and scarlet tunic, led them up the hill, with his sword flashing and his cloak streaming behind him. A bullet shattered his wrist, but Brock ignored the wound. Then, from behind a tree, an American sharpshooter took careful aim and Isaac Brock fell dead instantly. The shot struck Brock in the left breast and passed straight through his body.

Even in death Brock inspired his troops, who recalled his encouraging shout of "Push on, York volunteers!" as he had galloped ahead of them along the road to Queenston. Lieutenant-Colonel John Macdonnel took command and attempted another attack on the hill, but he was also shot to death. This left Major-General Roger Sheaffe in command of the defenders, and when he led a third attack to the west and behind the Americans, he successfully retook the Heights. The small force, yelling "Avenge the General!" beat the Americans back across the river. The British and Canadians lost 14 men but killed or wounded 300 and captured 958 prisoners.

By the end of the war not one metre of Canadian territory would be under American control. Isaac Brock's pledge "to keep the land inviolate" from U.S. invasion would be fulfilled.

## Deadly Duel

When Isaac Brock was only 21, an older officer in his regiment, who had already killed several rivals, taunted the young Brock into a pistol duel. When they arrived for the gentlemanly encounter, Brock, as the injured party, was allowed to dictate the terms of the contest. Rather than the customary 12 paces between them, Brock cocked his pistol and insisted that the duel be fought at point-blank range. His terms meant certain death for both men; the captain refused to fight and had to resign his commission in dishonour.

## Sobbing Sophie

When Isaac Brock died at Queenston Heights, he was a 46-year-old bachelor, but legend has it that he left behind his fiancée, Sophie Shaw, whom he had visited before the battle. She never married, and to this day it is said that the ghost of Sophie Shaw haunts her former house at present-day Niagara-on-the-Lake, where, on dark moonless nights, you can still hear the chilling sounds of a woman's lamenting wails.

## Natives and Blacks

The British regulars and the Lincoln and York militia won the Battle of Queenston Heights with the help of their native allies. The fiery and aggressive John Norton (Teyoninhokarawen) was born to a Scottish mother and Cherokee father, but he had been made a Mohawk war chief. His long black hair, tied together with a red handkerchief, was decorated with an ostrich feather, his face and body were painted for war, and he waved a deadly tomahawk. The warrior worked his way behind the American lines, leading 250 braves whose war whoops terrorized the U.S. troops. Beside him was John Brant, the 18-year-old son of the Mohawk chief, Joseph Brant, who had defended our borders and been granted a homeland here at the time of the American revolution.

Another group was Robert Runchey's platoon of black soldiers (runaway slaves from the southern United States who had found refuge in Canada). One of them, Private Richard Pierpont, nicknamed "Captain Dick," had proposed the small corps of about 30 men. They charged the enemy, sending some of the American invaders tumbling over the escarpment onto the rocks below.

## Massacre at River Raisin

In the last months of 1812, General Harrison, Commander-in-Chief of the Army of the Northwest, plundered and destroyed 19 native communities as Governor Isaac Shelby of Kentucky, with a dream of recapturing Fort Detroit, gathered over 2000 mounted militia and started out by exterminating native villages in Indiana and Illinois.

By January 18, 1813, General James Winchester, leading a large army of Kentucky troops, captured Frenchtown, just south of Detroit, from a small British force. Across the river from Detroit, at Fort Amherstburg (also known as Fort Malden), Colonel Henry Proctor launched a counterattack the next morning with fewer than 600 soldiers and about 500 warriors from such tribes as the Potawatomi, Miami, and Wyandot. He retook Frenchtown, killing or wounding 200 Kentuckians and capturing another 700; however, Proctor could not control his enraged native allies, who, eager to revenge the raids on their villages, pursued the retreating Kentucky soldiers along the frozen River Raisin, slaughtering and scalping hundreds of prisoners in the most hideous encounter of the war.

## Snowshoe Trek

Blankets of snow and ice-covered lakes put an end to hostilities during the winter months. Most of the American troops were not prepared for the harsh Canadian season, but in March 1813, 600 reinforcements from the 104th, a New Brunswick regiment, marched for 52 days on snowshoes from that province to Kingston, the Canadian shipbuilding headquarters of Commodore James Lucas Yeo. Rumours of their arrival thwarted a planned spring attack against Kingston.

## Make a Soldier's Hat

Soldiers on both sides during the War of 1812 wore tall, stiff felt hats called "shakos." (American shakos were also made of leather.) They were often decorated with brush-like plumes and brass plates to identify the regiment.

**What You Need:**
scissors, ruler, pencil
white glue
coloured pencils or crayons
scoring tool
several sheets of black construction paper

**What to Do*:**

1. Trace the rectangle and the circle on page 19 on to black construction paper and cut them out.

2. Apply glue to the long tab on the rectangle and glue it to the opposite side to form a cylinder.

3. Lightly score the tabs around the edge of the circle and fold them up. After the glued cylinder has dried completely, carefully push the circle down into the cylinder. Glue the tabs to the side of the cylinder.

4. Using the pattern on page 20 as a guide, trace the bill of the hat on to black paper. Glue the tabs on the bill around the front of the cylinder. (The seam is at the back.)

5. Cut out the brass plate. Colour it yellow and glue it to the front of the hat. Colour the plume red, and the centre of the medallion yellow. (Do not colour the back of the medallion.) Glue the plume above the brass plate. Your shako is now complete.

18

**\* Do not cut this book!**
Photocopy or trace pages 19 to 22.

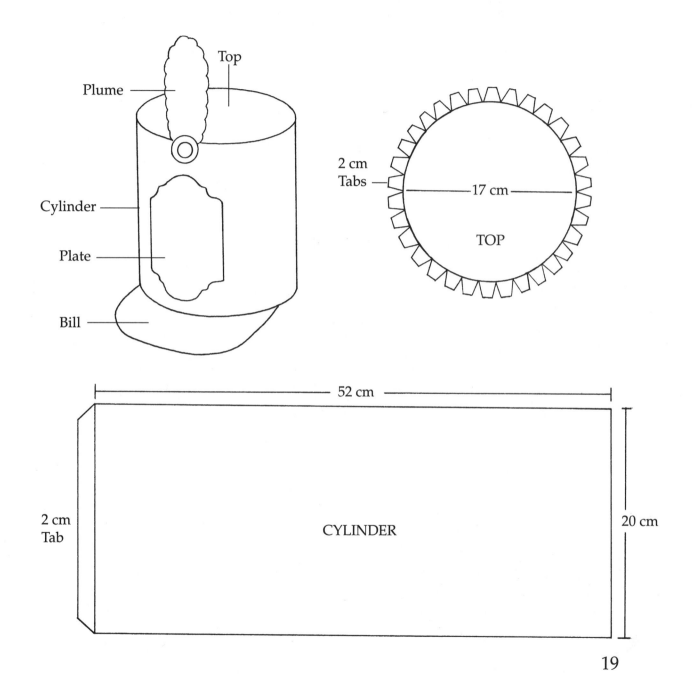

Plume

Top

Cylinder

Plate

Bill

2 cm
Tabs

17 cm

TOP

52 cm

2 cm
Tab

CYLINDER

20 cm

19

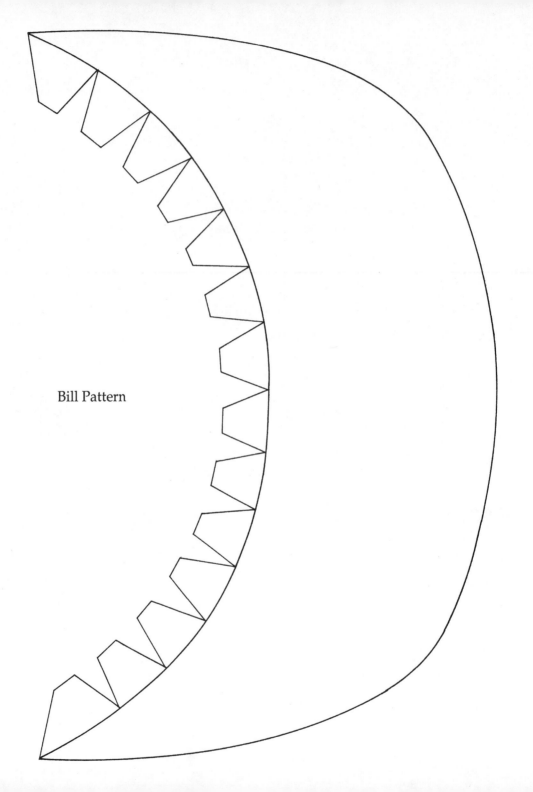

Bill Pattern

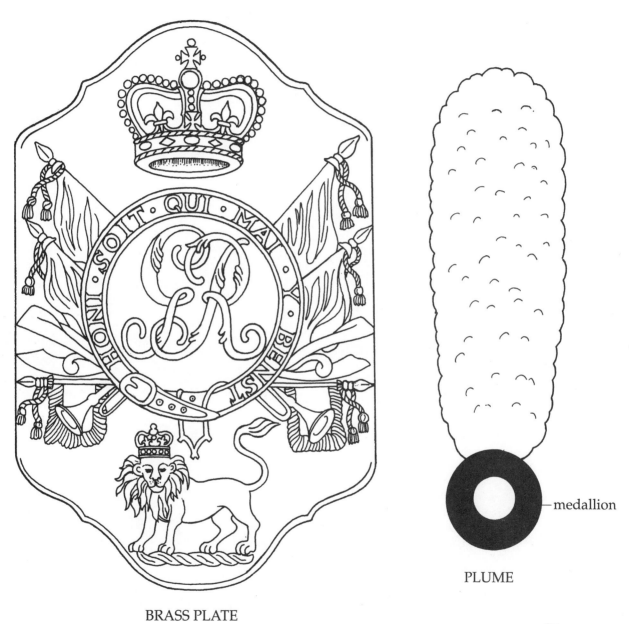

—medallion

PLUME

BRASS PLATE

21

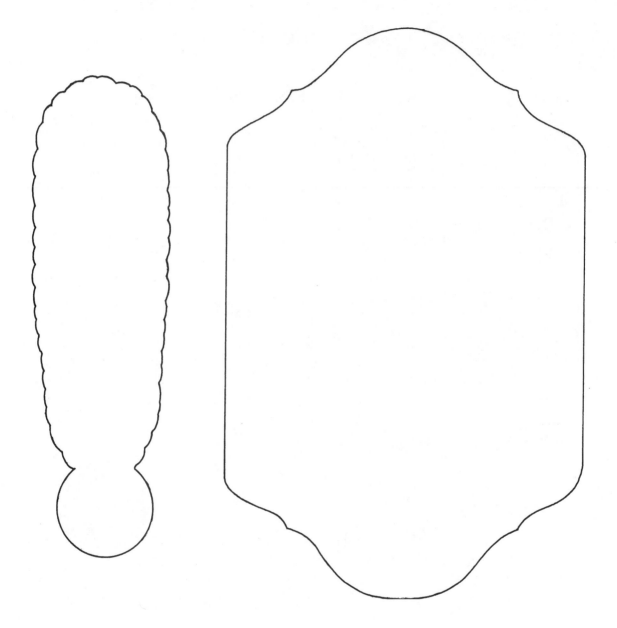

# 2 *Native Allies*

### *Tecumseh*

Without the support of the native people during the War of 1812, Canada might not exist today. There were many brave men from dozens of tribes who made significant contributions to the Canadian victories, but none more impressive than the powerful Shawnee chief, Leaping Panther.

Leaping Panther was born in 1768 in the Ohio Valley (near present-day Springfield) and grew up in the midst of warfare against white settlers. Before he was a teenager, he saw his father, who was a chief, shot by an American settler because the chief refused to act as a hunting guide. Following their father's death, Cheeseekau, Leaping Panther's older brother, took the youth on a three-year adventure, first hunting buffalo with the Osages and later fighting settlers with the Cherokees. By the time Cheeseekau was killed during a raid, Leaping Panther had earned the reputation of a great hunter and brave warrior, as well as the new name Tecumseh, which means "he moves from one spot to another."

Tecumseh also earned other reputations: as a man of mercy when he took a firm stand against the custom of torturing and killing prisoners; as an orator and leader when he and his younger brother, The Prophet, urged all the native tribes to join together and block the spread of American settlers into their treaty lands; as a lover when he romanced and proposed to Rebecca Galloway, the

16-year-old daughter of the white settler who introduced him to the Bible and Shakespeare; and as a politician when he bargained skillfully for native rights.

He became a chief and, in 1808, established the village of Prophet's Town on Tippecanoe Creek with his younger brother, where he tried to preserve the native culture, based on a peaceful agricultural life devoid of the destructive liquor introduced by the white men. After General Harrison attacked and destroyed Prophet's Town, Tecumseh gathered his native allies and moved north to Canada to join forces with the English and French settlers who were also being invaded by the United States. It had been his old friends, the British, who had granted the natives their treaty lands before the American revolution. He proclaimed: "Here is a chance — for us Indians of North America to form — into one great combination and cast our lot with the British in this war." His reputation as a warrior drew natives from many tribes, and their numbers grew to more than 1000.

Tecumseh's bravery and determination played an important part in the defence of Upper Canada, and the "bush telegraph" supplied by the natives brought advance news of American moves.

## Tecumseh Meets Brock

The two great leaders, Tecumseh and Isaac Brock, met face-to-face for the first time on the eve of the attack on General Hull at Fort Detroit. It was after midnight, as the general was studying his battle plans by candlelight, when the door burst open and revealed the famous Shawnee chief. Tecumseh was a handsome figure who stood 1.75 metres tall, with a soft oval face, firm straight nose, light reddish-brown skin, penetrating hazel eyes, and glistening white teeth.

His head was shaved bare, except for a dark, dangling scalp lock; hanging from his nose were three silver coronet-shaped objects and around his neck hung a colourful wampum belt with a huge silver medallion of King George III in the centre. He was dressed in a fringed, tanned deerskin jacket. From the regal appearance, Brock knew instinctively who the stranger was.

The general was dressed in his bright red jacket with white and blue pants and tall black boots. The two leaders surveyed each other for an instant and then spontaneously joined in a powerful handshake. Brock described Tecumseh as a "sagacious and gallant Warrior," claiming, "He was the admiration of everyone." Tecumseh simply told his followers, "This is a *man!*" Brock placed Tecumseh in command of Indian allies.

Tecumseh gave Brock a silk sash, and Brock reciprocated with a gift of his own sash and a pair of pistols.

## Tecumseh to the Rescue

On May 1, 1813, Henry Proctor, now a general, crossed from Fort Amherstburg (Fort Malden) and began four days of bombarding General Harrison and his army of 1200, sheltered inside Fort Meigs, with hundreds of cannon balls. About 1500 of Proctor's native allies surrounded the fort.

When General Green Clay arrived on May 5th with 1500 Kentucky troops to rescue the fort, they were defeated by the natives and 650 were captured. As the braves began to kill and scalp the prisoners, a re-enactment of the River Raisin massacre seemed inevitable, until Tecumseh rode onto the scene, roared angrily at the warriors, and saved the prisoners' lives.

# Forces in the War of 1812

## Sedentary Militia
In 1812, every Canadian male between the ages of 16 and 60 was expected to fight for his country, if required. These men were civilians, not properly trained for war. Most of them had no uniforms and would frequently be permitted to return, between battles, to tend to their farms or businesses. They usually wore their own civilian clothing.

## American Militia
The American state militia were basically loyal citizens fighting for their country. They wore grey uniforms and, in true democratic style, they sometimes elected their officers. Frequently during the war they refused to cross the Canadian border because they insisted that, under the terms of their enlistment, they were only required to protect their own borders, not invade another country.

Sometimes the American veterans of wars with the natives were as feared as any native warrior because of their practices of scalping and torturing their enemies.

The American regular army wore their traditional blue uniforms.

27

## Incorporated Militia of Upper Canada

These volunteers, sometimes as young as 14, were frequently from the patriotic families of United Empire Loyalists (former residents of the British colonies in the New England states who had moved to Canada after the U.S. revolution). Each new recruit who agreed to fight until the end of the war was given an enlistment bonus of 80 dollars.

## Militia in Lower Canada

The Select Embodied Militia of Lower Canada (Quebec), volunteer soldiers between the ages of 18 and 25, wore green jackets and were paid and trained the same as regular forces. They were sometimes rebellious young men, recruited from the slums of Quebec City and Montreal.

## Canadian Regular Units

Some of the professional soldiers were Canadian-born, serving in units such as the green-coated Glengarry Fencibles and the grey-clad Canadian Voltigeurs.

## British Regular Units

These professional soldiers wore the British scarlet tunics. Although most were sent from Britain, some Canadian recruits joined them. They were the backbone of our fighting forces in 1812 and included units such as the 41st and 49th regiments.

## The "Green Tigers"

This hand-selected company of infantry taken from the 49th regiment (referred to as the "Bloody Boys" on one occasion) followed James FitzGibbon, a towering leader, who had become a powerful legend. FitzGibbon called them his "Green Tigers" and in some battles these guerrilla fighters wore green uniforms to camouflage themselves.

## The Navy

When the United States declared war, it attacked British ships on the oceans. On August 19, 1812, the American frigate *Constitution* (Old Ironsides) conquered the British frigate *Guerrière* east of Boston. On October 29, the U.S. vessel *United States* captured Britain's *Macedonian*, and on December 29, the *Constitution* defeated *Java* off the coast of Brazil.

But by 1813, the British navy took back control of the high seas. When the British frigate *Shannon* eliminated the *Chesapeake*, the dying cry of the American captain, "Don't give up the ship!", became famous, although his ship was taken. On March 27, 1814, the British captured the *Essex* in the Pacific Ocean, off Chile, and later that year trapped the last American ship, *Constitution*, in port as a blockade of the entire Atlantic coast became effective.

Meanwhile, on the large interior lakes of North America, isolated naval battles were being fought as both sides busily built war ships in a race to control the inland waterways. The American shipbuilders on Lake Ontario were at Sackets Harbor, while the port of Kingston in Upper Canada was the main British base. On Lake Erie, the ships were built at Presque Isle in the U.S. and Amherstburg in Upper Canada. Both sides also built ships on Lake Champlain below Lower Canada. On some occasions, crowds of civilians gathered along the shores to witness the encounters, much like a sports contest today.

## The Dragoons

Among the most adventurous and romantic of the forces fighting in 1812 were the dragoons, musketeer-like horsemen galloping through the forest trails of Upper Canada, striking in raiding fashion at the enemy, often in the thick of night.

On the Canadian side were the Provincial Light Dragoons, led by young, 20-year-old William Merrit. They wore the blue uniform of the British dragoons, which could give them the advantage over confused opponents who mistook it for American blue. Frequently both sides, in order to keep warm, covered their uniforms with long grey overcoats in the "no-man's land" of the Niagara Peninsula, where you could never know who was friend and who was foe.

Their American equivalents were referred to as "Chapin's Savages," and their leader was Dr. Cyrenius Chapin.

## Canadian Volunteers

"King Joe" Willcock's 250 men, calling themselves "Canadian Volunteers," were mainly newly arrived settlers from the U.S.A. and others who sympathized with the American invasion. Their traitorous leader, "King Joe," had fought beside Isaac Brock at Queenston but changed sides when the Yankees captured and burnt York. They wore white badges and bands of green ribbons in their hats.

## Women

A limited number of wives and young children of soldiers were allowed to live in the forts and tents with their husbands, where they cooked, cleaned, and nursed.

During a battle, the women might run onto the field to pull wounded soldiers back to safety, and after a victory, they might collect any valuables or clothing from the bodies of the enemy.

If a woman's husband was killed during a battle, she and her children would be left without support. She would be sent back to Quebec or Montreal and supplied with rations for three months, at which point she had the choice of being shipped back to Britain or staying in Canada without rations.

## *Applying War Paint*

The assorted tribes that fought on both sides during the War of 1812 had clothing, war paint, and hair styles that were as distinct and traditional as the uniforms of the opposing armies. They would decorate their faces and bodies with war paint, partly to scare the enemy and partly to offer a magical protection to themselves during the fighting. Some braves covered their entire faces and bodies with black charcoal and white markings, other warriors stained themselves with red ochre, and still other natives preferred to smear on designs with blue clay.

**What You Need:**
A set of face paints from a toy or party supply store (the kind used for painting clown faces at birthday parties)

**What to Do:**

**1.** Think about the kinds of designs you wish to use. Indian warriors often used stripes and symmetrical shapes such as triangles, circles, and diamonds in their designs.

**2.** Apply the face paint following the instructions in the set.

**3.** Look at the others' faces! Who is the fiercest looking, the most serious, the funniest?

**4.** Clean up your faces and any mess you have made.

33

# CHAPTER 3 *Battle of the Lakes*

### *Sir James Lucas Yeo*

Whoever controlled the lakes and rivers would win the war. During the first year of the War of 1812, the Americans had suffered nothing but defeats. This was partly because the only reliable method of travel was by water. Canadian fur traders in express canoes moved rapidly down river routes with military dispatches and supplies, while the British navy controlled the Great Lakes. The few roads that did exist were dirt tracks through thick forests, which became mud holes in bad weather. All troops, cannons, and supplies had to travel by ship.

Without speedy transportation and communication, the Americans were at a disadvantage, but by 1813 that changed. The contest turned to shipbuilding. At Sackets Harbor the Yankees were busy constructing warships, and across Lake Ontario at Kingston and York, the Canadian shipbuilders were also working industriously.

On March 12, 1813, Sir James Yeo was appointed Commodore of the Royal Navy squadrons on the lakes. He was a slender, handsome, 30-year-old naval officer who, at only 15 years of age, had been promoted to lieutenant for merit. His U.S. counterpart, in command of the American fleet, was Commodore Chauncey, whose large guns gave him the advantage in calm weather at a long range; Yeo's ships were successful in rough weather at close quarters. The contest on Lake Ontario became a see-saw struggle between them.

# Burning of York

On April 26, 1813, Commodore Chauncey's American fleet of 14 ships, carrying a large invading army, sailed across Lake Ontario to attack York (present-day Toronto), the capital of Upper Canada. The official commanding general of the U.S. force was Henry Dearborn, who was nicknamed "Granny" by some of his own troops. He was frequently ill and so grossly overweight that he had trouble standing up. Sometimes it took several soldiers to help the 160-kg general into a boat or onto a horse. He stayed on his ship, sending Zebulon Pike, a new brigadier-general and famous American explorer (Pike's Peak) to lead the assault. Although it became the first U.S. victory of the war in Upper Canada, General Pike was killed when a York magazine exploded. There were 62 British and Canadians killed and 76 wounded; 300 Americans were killed or wounded.

The British officer, General Sheaffe, who had been victorious on Queenston Heights, withdrew his troops to the safety of Kingston, leaving a Scottish-born Canadian clergyman named John Strachan, who was an amateur soldier in the militia, to deal with the American terms of surrender.

Although the American army was generally respectful of private property, Dearborn was unable to control some of his militia. All night they plundered and burned the capital city of Upper Canada. The legislative building was set on fire; Strachan's church was looted. The lawlessness continued during a three-day occupation. When Chauncey heard that Commodore Yeo and the Canadian fleet were on their way from Kingston, the American army re-embarked and headed for an assault on Fort George, leaving Fort York destroyed and the government buildings in smouldering ashes.

## Capture of Fort George

After the burning and looting of York, the American army set sail for Fort George, which was defended by about 600 regular soldiers. On May 27, 1813, Major-General Dearborn attacked with about 3000 troops and 16 warships, commanded by Chauncey. As usual Dearborn stayed aboard ship and sent his second-in-command to lead the attack.

Defending the fort was Brigadier-General John Vincent, who, after a brief battle against such overwhelming odds, recognized defence was useless and that he would do better to save his men for another day. He ordered that his magazines be blown up and retreated, leaving the fort to the Americans.

One fearless young American officer, Colonel Winfield Scott, led the attack. He stomped out the burning fuses and was eager to chase the retreating redcoats, but Dearborn stopped him.

## Battle of Lake Erie

On September 10, 1813, Commodore Perry's new fleet of nine American ships moved out of Presque Isle to challenge the six vessels of the "One-Armed Captain," Robert Barclay, for the supremacy of Lake Erie. Perry had twice the firing power, but Barclay's guns had a longer range. The two fleets bombarded each other from morning to afternoon in a raging battle.

Perry's flag ship, *Lawrence*, was destroyed, but he rowed to another American brig, *Niagara*, took command away from Captain Elliott, who Perry believed had stayed out of the battle due to a personal grudge, and counterattacked, capturing the entire British fleet, including Barclay's ship, *Detroit*. Perry then ruled Lake Erie. He sent General Harrison the message: "We have met the enemy and they are ours."

BATTLE OF LAKE ERIE
September 10, 1813

BRITISH FRIGATE

40

# Lake Battles of the War

**April 26, 1813:** The U.S. fleet attacks and burns York (Toronto).

**May 16, 1813:** Commodore Yeo arrives at Kingston via Montreal with 150 men and sends Captain James Barclay, who had had one of his arms amputated, from Kingston to Amherstburg to command the Canadian fleet on Lake Erie.

**May 25, 1813:** U.S. reinforcements arrive to defend Sackets Harbor. Chauncey's squadron sails to Niagara, where the American fleet is bombarding Fort George on the Canadian side in preparation for an attack.

**May 27, 1813:** Chauncey's American fleet of 16 warships, with 3000 of Dearborn's soldiers against 600 defenders, attacks and captures Fort George. The British and Canadians retreat to Burlington Heights.

**May 29, 1813:** Victorious at Fort George, Chauncey rushes back to Sackets Harbor, where Yeo's fleet has attacked and landed 1200 troops at the U.S. naval base. He forces them to withdraw.

**June 1813:** The newly built British ship *Wolfe* gives the advantage to Yeo. The Canadians are the masters of Lake Ontario, for a while.

**July 20, 1813:** New U.S. ship *Pike* out on Lake Ontario.

**July 30, 1813:** U.S. fleet again attacks and burns York.

**August 2, 1813:** Yeo's squadron leaves Kingston and, at dawn on August 7, catches up to the American fleet at anchor off Niagara.

**August 8, 1813:** Two American ships, *Hamilton* and *Scourge*, are sunk in a sudden storm on Lake Ontario. It is the largest single loss of life on the lakes during the War of 1812.

**August 10, 1813:** Yeo captures two of Chauncey's schooners, *Julia* and *Growler*.

**End of August, 1813:** For two weeks the two squadrons pursue each other around Lake Ontario. Both *Wolfe* and *Pike* are damaged.

**September 10, 1813:** Battle of Lake Erie — American Commodore Perry wins a naval victory over Barclay. U.S. controls Lake Erie and re-takes Fort Detroit.

**End of April, 1814:** The British navy destroys or contains the entire U.S. navy on the Atlantic seaboard and imposes a blockade.

**August 14, 1814:** *St. Lawrence* is launched; Yeo takes control of Lake Ontario.

**August 24-25, 1814:** In retaliation for the burning of York, the British fleet on the Atlantic attacks and burns Washington.

**September 3-6, 1814:** Canadians at Mackinac Island (Fort Michilimackinac) capture American vessels *Tigress* and *Scorpion*, taking control of Lake Huron.

**September 10, 1814:** Battle of Lake Champlain. American fleet is victorious.

## Merchant or Pirate?

Halifax-born Samuel Cunard was the son of a carpenter who became a millionaire and founder of one of the most famous ship-building companies in the world. During the War of 1812, the 25-year-old merchant convinced the lieutenant-governor of Nova Scotia to allow him to trade with the American enemy settlements on the Atlantic coast. At the same time, he backed a Nova Scotian privateer who captured and plundered Yankee ships.

## Death of Tecumseh

When the British fleet was captured on Lake Erie, the red coats and their native allies were forced to retreat from Detroit to Moraviantown on the Thames River in Upper Canada. It was there, at the Battle of the Thames, that a British force of 900 under General Proctor and 500 natives led by Tecumseh attempted to hold off Harrison's advancing American army of 3500 soldiers on October 5, 1813.

The battle was lost before it began. Tecumseh told his braves: "Brother warriors, we enter an engagement today from which I shall not return." He was killed during the battle, as he predicted.

Although allies, Proctor and Tecumseh were not friends. The native leader called Proctor "a running dog" for retreating from Detroit. Proctor, whose weakness as a leader had been partly responsible for the Raisin River slaughter, ran for his life after his defeat on the Thames, fearful of the dreaded Kentucky troops, whose rallying cry was "Remember River Raisin!" He was disgraced, court martialled, and suspended.

## Tying Ships' Knots

A knowledge of which knots to use for different jobs was part of every sailor's training. The well-being of his ship and the lives of the crew depended on this skill.

**What You Need:**
Three pieces of rope about 1 to 1.5 metres long. Two of these should be of the same thickness (about 1.5 cm), the other a little thinner (about 1 cm).

**What to Do:**
Follow the instructions on the next two pages to learn to tie these sailors' knots. There are many other useful ships' knots; these are only a few.

**1.** THE SQUARE KNOT is the most common knot used for tying together two ropes of the same thickness. It is easy to untie.

**2.** THE SHEET BEND is used for tying together two ropes of different thickness.

**3.** THE BOWLINE is a very important knot. It forms a loop that will not slip. It is used for fastening a boat to a post at piers.

**4.** TWO HALF HITCHES is used for tying a rope to a pole.

**5.** THE TIMBER HITCH is used for dragging logs.

SQUARE KNOT

SHEET BEND

44

BOWLINE

TWO HALF HITCHES          TIMBER HITCH

# 4 *Teenage Courage*

### *Billy Green*

Although it is ambitious politicians and old generals who often provoke wars, it is frequently young men and innocent boys who fight and die in them. The War of 1812 was no different. Many of the troops on both sides were teenagers, some as young as 14 or 15.

In the spring of 1813, the new American offensive was threatening to take the Niagara Peninsula and all of Upper Canada. York had been attacked and burned, Fort George and Fort Erie were captured, Queenston was occupied, and 3000 Americans were advancing by land towards a cluster of defenders, Vincent's small force of 700 regulars grouped on the heights overlooking Burlington Bay (Hamilton).

It is said that teenager Billy Green, the youngest of seven brothers and sisters, was familiar with the thick forests on the Niagara Escarpment where he had grown up hunting and fishing. He could move through the dense wilderness around his family's hillside cabin above the village of Stoney Creek with speed and stealth.

As the Americans marched through the tiny settlement of Stoney Creek, they took Billy's brother-in-law, Isaac Corman, prisoner. Later Isaac convinced the American major that he was sympathetic to the U.S. invasion, and thus he was not only released, but given the countersign of the day to identify himself as a friend in case

other U.S. soldiers challenged him on the road home to Stoney Creek. The password was an abbreviated version of the name of the American general, William Henry Harrison, "Wil Hen Har." When Isaac told Billy, the bright youth realized immediately that the information would be useful to the British and Canadian troops at Burlington.

First on his horse, Tip, and then by foot, Billy rushed with his news to Lieutenant-Colonel John Harvey. Harvey had already decided on a surprise night raid against the American troops, so the countersign was invaluable. When Billy announced that he also knew the trail to the Yankee camp, Harvey gave him a corporal's sword and invited him to lead the way. Billy escorted the Canadian forces 11 km through the dark forests in the middle of the night.

Armed with the secret password and his new sword, Billy took out the first U.S. sentry when they reached the sleeping American camp. Then bedlam broke out as musket and cannon fire echoed with native war whoops and the screams of the dying. In the dark confusion, soldiers were firing on their comrades, and the British commander, Vincent, got separated and lost. When dawn arrived, the Americans were on the run. One hundred were captured, including the U.S. commanding officer, Brigadier-General John Chandler, his second-in-command, William Winder, and four of their six cannons.

From the safety of the captured Fort George, Dearborn ordered a second wave of soldiers under Morgan Lewis to attack again at Stoney Creek, but when Sir James Yeo and the British fleet appeared at the mouth of the Niagara River, Dearborn hastily sent a new message to Morgan to quickly return to help defend the fort. Yeo's fleet moved up to the Forty Mile Creek and captured all of Lewis's deserted supplies.

LIGHT
ARTILLERY
CANNON

Up until the Battle of Stoney Creek and the heroism of 19-year-old Billy Green, the Canadians were preparing to evacuate the Niagara Peninsula and retreat to Kingston. Now, having beaten a force three times their size, the Canadians were again on the attack. The Americans abandoned and burnt Fort Erie as they retreated in confusion from their posts on the Niagara River. That winter they would also be forced to leave Fort George and return to American soil.

## Butter Peddler

Before the Battle of Stoney Creek, James FitzGibbon of the "Green Tigers" disguised himself as a butter peddler and wandered freely amongst the American troops, selling his wares as he spied on their numbers and strength. He bragged later, "I got a good price for it!"

# Land Battles of the War

**June 18, 1812:** The United States declares war.
1. **July 12, 1812:** General Hull invades Canada.
2. **July 16, 1812:** Captain Roberts captures Fort Michilimackinac on Mackinac Island.
3. **August 16, 1812:** General Hull surrenders Fort Detroit.
4. **October 13, 1812:** Battle of Queenston Heights. Death of Brock.
5. **January 19, 1813:** Massacre at River Raisin.
6. **February 22, 1813:** Capture of Ogdensburg, New York.
7. **April 26, 1813:** General Dearborn attacks and burns York.
8. **May 5, 1813:** Proctor and Tecumseh attack Fort Meigs.
9. **May 27, 1813:** General Dearborn captures Fort George.
10. **June 5, 1813:** Battle of Stoney Creek.
11. **June 21, 1813:** Battle of Beaver Dams.
12. **October 5, 1813:** Battle of the Thames.
13. **October 25, 1813:** Battle of Châteauguay.
14. **November 11, 1813:** Battle of Crysler's Farm.
15. **July 5, 1814:** Battle of Chippawa.
16. **July 25, 1813:** Battle of Lundy's Lane.
17. **August 14, 1814:** General Drummond's attack on Fort Erie.
18. **October 19, 1814:** Battle of Cook's Mills.
19. **September 11, 1814:** Battle of Lake Champlain.
**December 24 1814:** Treaty of Ghent ends the war.
**January 8, 1815:** Battle of New Orleans.

50

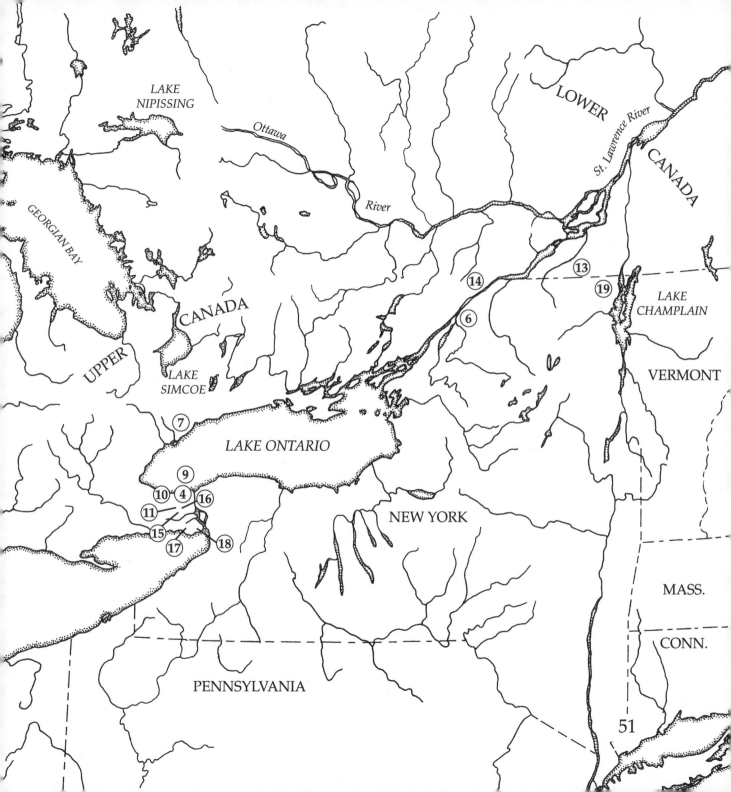

LAKE
NIPISSING

Ottawa

River

LOWER

St. Lawrence River

CANADA

GEORGIAN BAY

CANADA

UPPER

⑬

⑭

⑥

⑲

LAKE
CHAMPLAIN

VERMONT

LAKE
SIMCOE

⑦

LAKE ONTARIO

⑨

⑩ ④ ⑯

⑪

⑮

⑰

⑱

NEW YORK

MASS.

CONN.

PENNSYLVANIA

51

## *Play Siege (an 1812 War Game)*

### Object:
The **attacker** must remove all of the **defenders** without losing all of his or her own soldiers within 30 moves. If any soldiers remain in the fort, it will have been "relieved" and the defenders victorious, even if there are soldiers remaining outside.

### What You Need:
a die (one of a pair of dice)
35 defending "soldiers"
70 attacking "soldiers"
(You can colour toothpicks or use small pieces of paper to make soldiers.)

### What to Do:
1. Use photocopies of the fort on page 53, or a small bowl and toothpicks.

2. Pace 35 defending soldiers in the fort.

3. Place 70 attacking soldiers around the outside of the fort.

4. The attacker throws the die first. The defender then throws the die. The difference between the two is subtracted from the soldiers of the player with the lowest throw.

**Example:** The attacker throws 6, and the defender throws 4. Two soldiers are taken out of the fort or crossed out on the score card. (You can record the rolls of the die on the score card on page 54.)

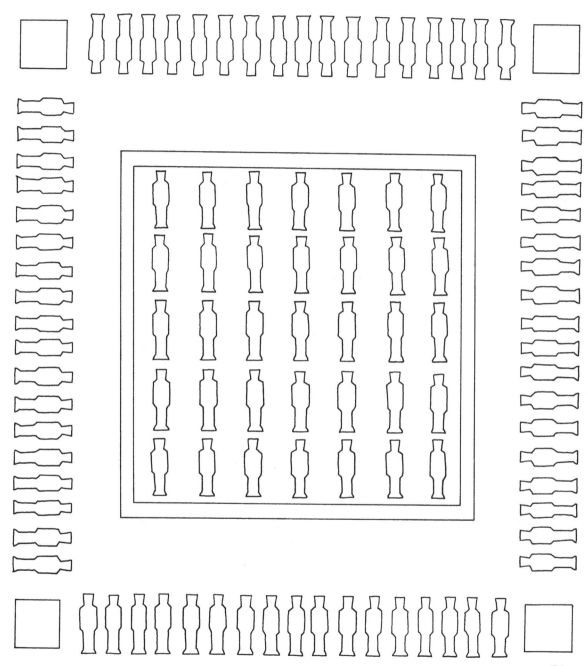

53

# Score Card

## 1812 War Song

### The Chesapeake and the Shannon

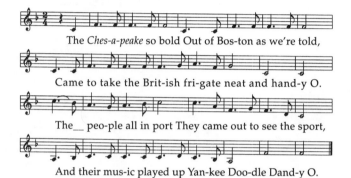

The Ches-a-peake so bold Out of Bos-ton as we're told,

Came to take the Brit-ish fri-gate neat and hand-y O.

The__ peo-ple all in port They came out to see the sport,

And their mus-ic played up Yan-kee Doo-dle Dand-y O.

Before this action it begun
The Yankees made much fun
Saying, "We'll tow her up to Boston neat and handy O;
And after that we'll dine,
Treat our sweethearts all with wine,
And we'll dance a jig of Yankee Doodle Dandy O. "

Our British frigate's name
All for the purpose came
In so cooling Yankee's courage neat and handy O.
Was the *Shannon*, Captain Brookes,
And his crew all hearts of oaks,
And in fighting they were allowed to be the dandy O.

The action scarce begun
When they flinched from their guns,
They thought they had worked us neat and handy O;
But Brookes he wove his sword,
Saying, "Come, my boys, we'll board,
And we'll stop this playing up Yankee Doodle Dandy O."

When Britons heard this word
They all sprang on board;
They hauled down the Yankee's ensign neat and handy O.
Notwithstanding all their brags
The British raised their flags
On the Yankee's mizzen-peak was quite the dandy O.

Brookes and all his crew
In courage stout and true
They worked the Yankee frigate neat and handy O.
O may they ever prove
In fighting or in love
That the bold British tars will be the dandy O!

**5** *Heroine of Upper Canada*

### *Laura Secord*

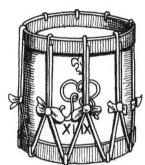

When we think about wars in the past, we usually imagine brave and daring young heroes fighting for their countries, yet one of our most famous personalities from the War of 1812 was a middle-aged heroine who was the mother of five.

Laura Secord was born in 1775 in the British colony of Massachusetts, but after the American revolution against the British, like many thousands of citizens still loyal to the Crown who were called United Empire Loyalists, she moved north with her family and settled in Upper Canada. Her father, Thomas Ingersoll, had been left with four girls when his first wife died. Laura, at eight years of age, was the eldest and thus from an early age was expected to take much of the responsibility in raising her younger sisters. The expectations increased when her father remarried and the family grew larger. Thomas was given a land grant (the present site of Ingersoll, Ontario) and opened a tavern at Queenston, where Laura ran the business and met James Secord. The young couple married in 1798, and until the war broke out in 1812, life was good for them. They had five children, two servants, a pleasant frame house, and a prosperous store, which carried household appliances and women's wear.

During the Battle of Queenston Heights, word came to Laura that her husband, who was fighting as a sergeant on the Canadian side, lay wounded on the battlefield, calling her name. She rushed up the Heights, searching frantically among the corpses until she finally discovered him on the side of a cliff. He was wounded in the knee and arm, unable to flee. His shoulder was bleeding badly, so Laura tore a piece of cloth from her petticoat, which she pressed against the wound to stop the flow of blood. Myth has it that, as she comforted her husband, three American soldiers approached, killing wounded Canadians as they lay helpless on the battlefield. One of the soldiers raised his rifle butt over James' head, but Laura threw herself across her defenceless husband, begging the men to kill her instead. As the surprised soldiers hesitated, an American officer, Captain Wool, arrived and ordered his men to allow Laura to take James back to Queenston, where their home had been ransacked and everything of value looted from their store.

In May of 1813, the Americans occupied Queenston during a new effort to overrun Upper Canada. The Secords and their five children were confined to the kitchen and one small bedroom in their own home because American officers took over the house.

It became the habit of the officers to sit around the dining table, after Laura had fed them their dinner, and discuss the war. On June 21, a special guest ate with the others — Colonel Boerstler, the commander of the U.S. forces at Queenston. After supper, the Secords listened secretly as Dr. Cyrenius Chapin, the leader of the Yankee dragoons, described a plan to lead a surprise attack against Lieutenant-Colonel FitzGibbon's "Green Tigers," at Beaver Dams. A victory would give the Americans control of all the Niagara Peninsula.

Someone had to warn FitzGibbon, and since James was still unable to walk due to his wounded leg, Laura insisted on carrying the news. She slipped away in the middle of the night. To avoid

LAURA SECORD

59

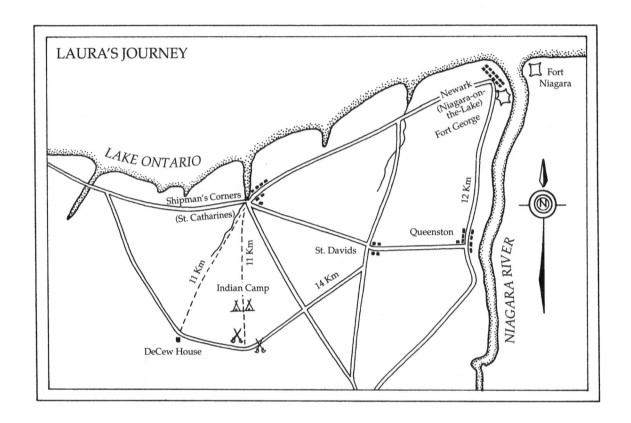

LAURA'S JOURNEY

American soldiers, she travelled deep into hostile forests filled with rattlesnakes, wolves, and wildcats. By morning she had arrived at St. David's, where she was joined by her teenaged niece, Elizabeth, but the young girl was forced to stop later, due to exhaustion. It was a strenuous hike but the 38-year-old Mrs. Secord continued alone through black swamps and dense thickets despite the hot summer sun beating down; her shoes were worn and her feet cut and swollen.

She reached Shipman's Corners (present-day St. Catharines) and started out again for DeCew House, James FitzGibbon's headquarters, which was still 11 kilometres away. As night approached, she crawled across Twelve Mile Creek on a fallen tree, but then she stopped, horrified. From the forest, ferociously painted natives carrying tomahawks closed in a circle around her. She had stumbled into their camp. Although she was aware that they probably were part of the native forces fighting with FitzGibbon against the Americans, she was still a white women alone in the wilderness and she was terrified. Because she had arrived from the direction of the enemy lines, they were suspicious that she was a spy. Her courage and persistence convinced the chief to take her to FitzGibbon, as she demanded.

Eighteen hours and 32 kilometres after she began her journey, Laura was ushered into the presence of James FitzGibbon and uttered in an exhausted voice the news of the surprise attack the Americans would be launching. FitzGibbon described Laura as a woman with "a strong and persistent will" and later credited her with the victory that followed when his small group of 44 Green Tigers and Dominique Ducharme's native band ambushed and captured a larger American force at Beaver Dams, ensuring that the Niagara Peninsula remained Canadian territory. Laura returned secretly behind enemy lines to her family, without anyone learning of her heroic journey until long after the war.

A LONG-HANDLED GRIDDLE

## Battle of Beaver Dams

In June of 1813, General Dearborn ordered Colonel Charles Boerstler to lead a secret attack on John DeCew's farmhouse, near Beaver Dams. It was known to be the headquarters of the Canadian, British, and native guerillas: William Merritt's Provincial Dragoons, FitzGibbon's "Green Tigers" (sometimes referred to as "The Bloody Boys" by historians), John Norton's Mohawks, and, recently, a band of Caughnawaga natives from Lower Canada (Quebec) under their French-speaking leader, Dominique Ducharme.

Including 500 men, two cannons, and Dr. Cyrenius Chapin's mounted infantry, Boerstler's attack force marched in the dead of night, reaching St. David's by sunrise on June 24, 1813. When the Americans scaled the Niagara Escarpment, they encountered Dominique Ducharme's Caughnawagans waiting in ambush in the thick forest, and three hours of fighting began.

In the midst of the chaotic encounter, James FitzGibbon appeared under a flag of truce with 44 of his seasoned Green Tigers, demanding an American surrender. It was merely a bluff, but FitzGibbon convinced Colonel Boerstler that there was a large British regular army concealed in the woods, rather than the few natives and his own small company. Thus, the Colonel surrendered his 500 soldiers and Chapin's marauding raiders. Laura Secord's warning, Dominique Ducharme's ambush, and James FitzGibbon's hoax had worked.

When General Dearborn, back in the safety of the captured Fort George, heard of the defeat at Beaver Dams, he was both shocked and furious. The defeats at Stoney Creek and Beaver Dams forced him to give up his command, and he was replaced by General James Wilkinson.

## Smugglers

Long after the war, in 1835, James Secord had become a collector of customs at Chippawa. One night he needed another man to help him arrest two smugglers, but no one would volunteer. Laura, more than 60 years old, threw on a long overcoat, pulled a hat down over her ears, grabbed a gun, and helped her husband capture the criminals.

## Poverty and Old Age

When her husband, James, died in 1841, Laura was left without an income. In those days there was no insurance for wives, no social security, no old-age pensions. She turned to needlework and opened a school in her cottage to earn money for food. When Laura asked for his help, James FitzGibbon of the Green Tigers came to her rescue, revealing her role in the Battle of Beaver Dams, and in 1860, when Laura was 85, the visiting Prince of Wales (later King Edward VII) recognized her heroic 32-km trek with a cash reward of 100 pounds. She died at the age of 93.

## Chocolates

Today "Laura Secord" is mainly associated with a Canadian chocolate company that uses her name. You can make your own chocolate treats for classmates and friends by following an old family chocolate fudge recipe, supplied by Vicky Kosharewich, on the opposite page.

# Victoria's 1812 Chocolate Fudge Recipe

*What You Need:*
*2/3 cup (150 ml) cocoa*
*3 cups (750 ml) sugar*
*1 and 1/2 cups (375 ml) heavy cream*
*a candy thermometer*
*a heavy saucepan*
*a 20-cm (8-inch) pan, lightly buttered*
*nuts (optional)*

*What to Do:*
*1. Combine the cocoa, sugar, and cream in a heavy saucepan, mixing well.*
*2. Then, on medium heat, bring them to a rolling boil.*
*3. Now, reduce heat — DO NOT STIR — and cook until mixture reaches 112 degrees Celsius (234 degrees Fahrenheit). Use a candy thermometer (soft-ball stage).*
*4. Cook until lukewarm, 34 degrees Celsius (110 degrees Fahrenheit).*
*5. Now, beat until thick.*
*6. You may add nuts of your choice at this point (optional).*
*7. Spread in the lightly buttered 20-cm (8-inch) pan.*
*8. When cool, cut into squares.*

# 6 *Defending Lower Canada*

### *Lieutenant-Colonel de Salaberry*

When the Americans invaded Canada, they expected to be welcomed as liberators by the French-Canadian habitants of Lower Canada (Quebec) and the yeomen (farmers and settlers) of Upper Canada (Ontario). However, the Canadians remained loyal to the British crown.

As 1813 ended, the snow-covered forest roads and freezing lakes soon made troop movements impossible until the spring of 1814. The Americans had burned York, captured Fort George, taken control of Lake Erie, won the Battle of the Thames, and had assembled three large armies ready to strike north.

The U.S. Army of the Northwest, under General Harrison, was forced to retreat south by the approaching winter. The army of the centre was now under the command of Major-General James Wilkinson, since General Dearborn had been replaced after being disgraced at Stoney Creek and Beaver Dams. The Canadians and British at Burlington Heights were posing a threat to the Americans on the Niagara Peninsula. A third U.S. army in northern New York State was led by Major-General Wade Hampton.

In the declining months of 1813, the Americans decided to invade Lower Canada (present-day province of Quebec) and capture Montreal. General Hampton's army would advance north; General Wilkinson's would move east along the St. Lawrence.

QUEBEC MILITIA FLAG

## Battle of Châteauguay

General Hampton, a plantation owner from South Carolina, owned thousands of slaves and had brought some of them to serve his needs as his army of 4000 blue-clad regular troops, along with 1500 grey-uniformed militia, advanced north.

Preparing to defend Lower Canada was a force of about 1600 British, Canadians, and natives. The defenders were a colourful assortment: British Regulars, Canadian Voltigeurs (French-Canadian troops decked out in bearskin hats and grey uniforms with black trim); Canadian Fencibles (Canadian regular infantry in bright red coats); Sedentary Militia (wearing homemade shirts and blue toques); militia from Lower Canada (Quebec) sporting green jackets with red trim; Select Embodied Militia (scarlet-coated French-Canadian and Scottish farmers from Upper Canada led by "Red George" Macdonnel); and Dominique Ducharme's Caughnawaga natives, returned from their victory at Beaver Dams.

On October 25, 1813, the advancing U.S. army clashed with 300 Canadian militia, dug in behind ravine barriers on the Châteauguay River, commanded by a bold, French-Canadian colonel, Charles-Michel de Salaberry, who had been a soldier since 14, and had a jagged bullet scar across his cheek from a personal duel. To disguise his small numbers, de Salaberry sent a few dozen natives shouting through the forests, creating the impression that there were hundreds of them. "Red George's" men appeared at the edge of the woods in scarlet jackets, ducked back, reversed their coats so that they were white, and reappeared as if they were a different group. Buglers stationed throughout the woods sounded the attack.

General Hampton was fooled into believing there was a huge Canadian force and ordered all his 5500 troops to retreat back across the border; less than 500 Canadians had been involved in the fight.

## Battle of Crysler's Farm

In early November of 1813, the central American army, under General Wilkinson, moved toward Montreal from Sackets Harbor, via Grenadier Island, and east along the St. Lawrence. Thousands of men in 350 boats formed an impressive five-mile procession with fluttering flags, sparkling weapons, and beating drums.

Their euphoria was shattered when Canadian snipers and cannons opened fire along the bush-covered river banks and British gun boats appeared on their heels. Nevertheless, Wilkinson's troops continued to the deadly Long Sault rapids. Near John Crysler's farm, 2500 American troops turned to deal with a small force that had been harassing their rear. Lieutenant-Colonel Morrison was the British commander of two regiments: the 89th, newly arrived from England in their neat, red jackets, and Isaac Brock's old regiment, the 49th, wearing grey winter overcoats over their uniforms. He also had some Canadian Fencibles,

Voltigeurs, and natives, but his force of 800 was drastically out-numbered against the 8000-man American army that he was shadowing.

Morrison had planned his defences with all the conventional wisdom and precision of British field tactics. His troops were trained to follow commands and fire deafening volleys in unison. The U.S. troops were experienced fighters in bush battles against native foes but were used to firing independently and randomly.

On November 11, the 2500 Americans clashed with the defenders, but the U.S. force mistook the grey-clad 49th for untrained militia and were destroyed by the organized, professional defences that they encountered. When the smell of powder and thick clouds of grey smoke cleared, Morrison was victorious. The huge American army proceeded to Cornwall, but heard of General Hampton's defeat at Châteauguay, and retreated back to American soil. Lower Canada was saved from invasion.

## Create an Army

**What You Need:**
scissors
white glue
scoring tool
coloured pencils or crayons

**What to Do:**
**Do not colour or cut this book!\***

**1.** Photocopy the following pages, then colour the soldiers as follows:

**British soldiers:** black hats, red coats, white straps, white pants, black shoes.

**American soldiers:** black hats, dark blue coats, white straps, white pants, black shoes.

**2.** Cut out the soldiers. Fold back the A folds and glue the bottoms of the base together.

**3.** Fold forward the B folds and apply glue **to one side only** of the figure and glue the two sides of the figure together.

\* photocopy these pages as many times as you wish to make as large an army as you desire.

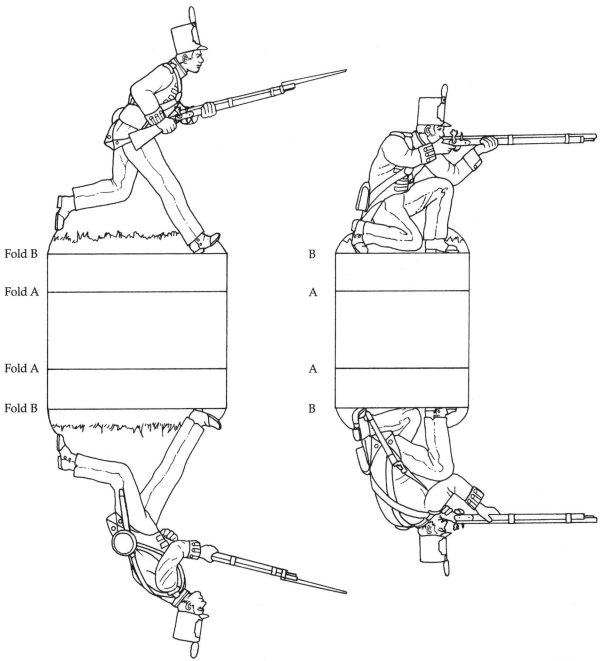

Fold B

Fold A

Fold A

Fold B

B

A

A

B

73

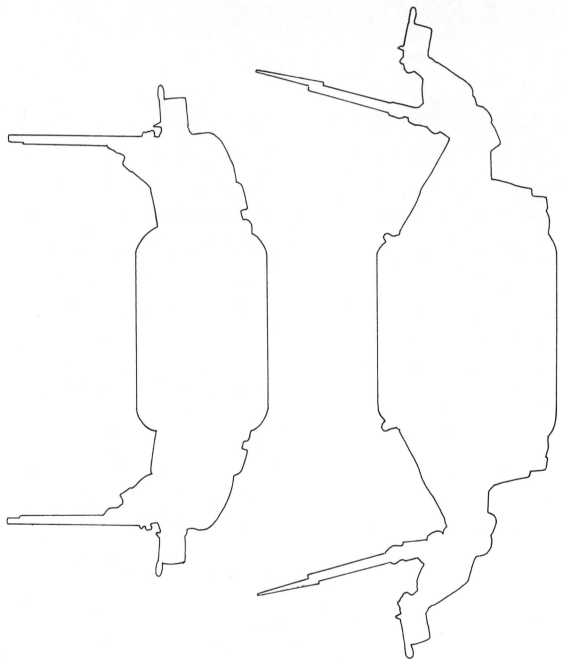

74

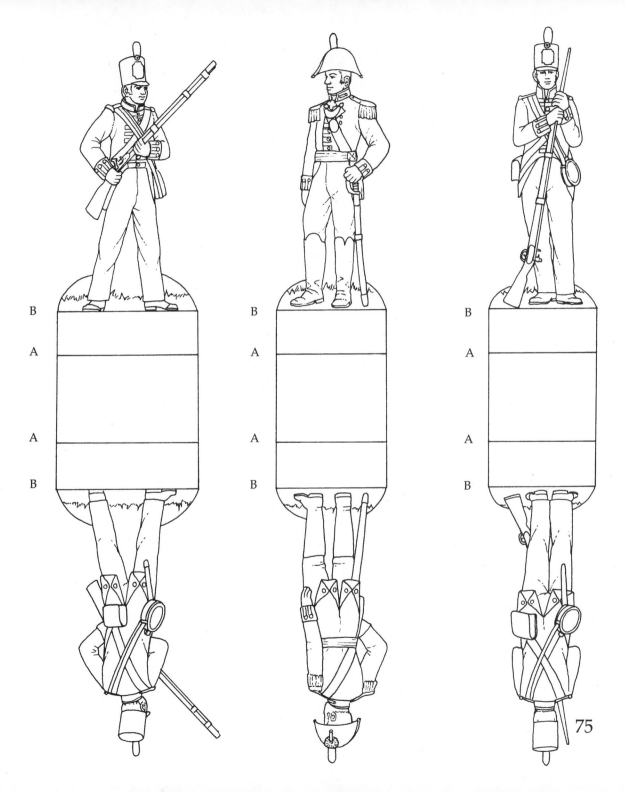

B

A

A

B

B

A

A

B

B

A

A

B

75

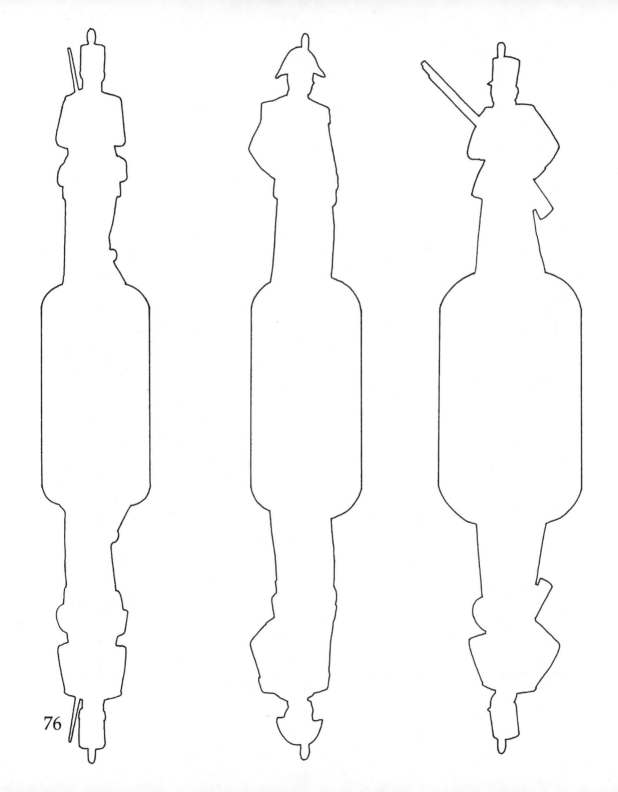

76

# 7 *The Final Invasion*

## *General Drummond*

The third and bloodiest year of the war began in the spring of 1814. The new leader of the U.S. army was Major-General Jacob Brown and the new lieutenant-general in charge of the defending British forces was Canadian-born Gordon Drummond.

The closing months of 1813 had not been good for the U.S. Both invading armies were defeated and forced to retreat after the battles of Châteauguay and Crysler's Farm. In addition, the hostility of the British troops, loyal Canadian citizens, native peoples, and mounted dragoons on the Niagara Peninsula kept the U.S. troops confined to Fort George until they were forced to abandon it. In retreating, they needlessly burnt and plundered the defenceless Canadian town of Newark (present-day Niagara-on-the-Lake), which contained only women and children. That act enraged the defenders. They retaliated by crossing the river, capturing Fort Niagara, and burning the communities of Black Rock, Lewiston, Youngstown, Manchester (Niagara Falls), and Buffalo in December 1813.

In the far north, the Canadians still held Fort Michilimackinac and controlled all the surrounding territories. When U.S. general William Clark captured Prairie du Chien on the Upper Mississippi, Colonel Robert McDouall sent a force to recapture it. When the Yankees mounted an attack on Fort Michilimackinac, McDouall pushed them back. When American schooners *Tigress* and *Scorpion* set up a blockade designed to starve the defenders into surrendering Fort Michilimackinac, a daring night raid took place. Using canoes, members of the Royal Newfoundland Regiment (East Coast fishermen and sailors sent to help defend the fort) and Robert Dickson's natives ("The Flaming-Haired Man") boarded and, after a hand-to-hand fight, captured *Tigress*. A few days later, on September 5, they used their prize to quietly approach and take the unsuspecting *Scorpion*, thus ensuring the Canadians complete control of Lake Huron and the entire northwest by September 1813.

## Battle of Chippawa

In the summer of 1814, General Brown began a new invasion of Upper Canada. With the British and Canadians back in control of Fort George and occupying Fort Niagara on the American side, he captured Fort Erie. His plan was to march by land up the Niagara Peninsula, take Burlington Heights, occupy York (Toronto), and move on to Kingston with his army of 3500.

General Drummond sent a large number of troops to block his American rival's route. The two forces met for the first time on July 5, 1814, just beyond the only bridge over the Chippawa River. The Battle of Chippawa was a deadly clash. When the noise and mayhem had subsided, the Americans were victorious and more than 800 brave men from both sides had been killed.

The American hero of the encounter was again Winfield Scott, now a general, whose regular soldiers had been sent grey militia uniforms, rather than the traditional blue ones, which were not available. Because of his impressive victory at Chippawa, the cadets at West Point later honoured him by adopting his grey uniforms as their official dress.

ATTACK ON THE *TIGRESS*

## Battle of Lundy's Lane

Following the defeat at Chippawa, General Drummond rushed reinforcements to the area and arrived to command the defenders himself, this time assembling his troops around Cemetery Hill (now Drummond Hill) on Lundy's Lane, the main road leading from the Niagara Falls area towards Burlington Heights.

When the Americans attacked on July 25, 1814, it was the most devastating battle of the war in Upper Canada. At different times each side appeared to be winning; the confusion and destruction seemed endless; both generals were wounded. Brown, hit with a musket ball in his right leg and a spent cannon ball against his body, was forced to give up his command to one of his subordinates. Drummond, blood gushing from a neck wound, pushed aside one of his aids, who was trying to force him to safety to receive treatment, and rallied his battered soldiers for a last charge. Participating in most battles since August 1813 were the British "Rocketeers," whose Congreve rockets illuminated the skies. The encounter ended with the Americans in charge of the hill, but there was a grotesque spectacle — intermingled piles of mangled corpses in blue, red, and grey uniforms. Drummond had lost 880 men; the American casualties were 860. Brown retreated to Chippawa.

## Attack on Fort Erie

By August 14, 1814, Drummond had chased the Yankees into the protection of Fort Erie, their last foothold in Canada. Each army had about 3000 soldiers. In a failed attempt to storm the fort, Drummond's young nephew was killed and more than 900 troops died.

When General Brown counterattacked on September 17, another staggering loss of life occurred on both sides; 511 Americans and 565 Canadians or British became casualties.

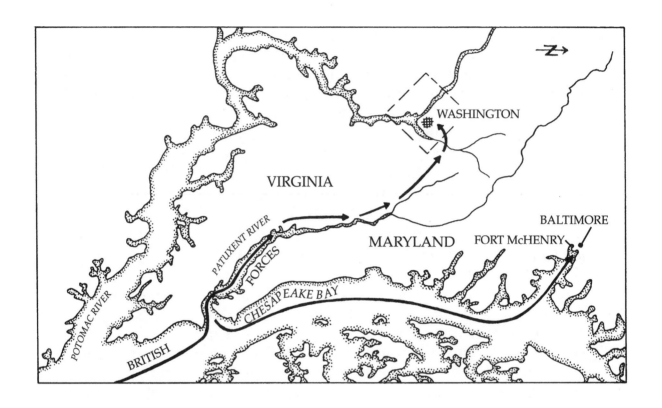

## Burning of Washington (August 24, 1814)

By August, British ships had blockaded the Atlantic coast of the United States and eliminated the American navy. They finally had the opportunity to avenge the burning of York, the capital of Upper Canada. They landed an army and marched on the American capital, Washington, D.C. While President Madison hid for his life, his home, government buildings, and city were burned. According to legend, the scorched mansion of the president later had to be white-washed, thus creating the White House.

## Battle of Lake Champlain (September 10, 1814)

By the summer of 1814, England had defeated the French in Europe and could finally spare some of Wellington's veteran troops to reinforce the Canadian colonies. General George Prevost, with a huge army of 11,000, marched south from Montreal into New York State. For a change, it was the Americans who were the defenders and outnumbered. As the Canadians had done so often in the first years of the war, the Yankees at Plattsburgh deceived General Prevost into believing that their small numbers were a huge army. When his fleet on Lake Champlain was destroyed and captured by the American commodore, Thomas Macdonough, Prevost retreated back to Lower Canada. Later, when a naval inquiry seemed to criticize his role in the battle, Prevost requested a court martial to clear his name, but died one month before it was to take place in 1815.

## Battle of Cook's Mills and the "Super Ship"

On September 28, a fresh U.S. army of 4000 experienced fighters arrived at Fort Erie. The Yankees made a final invasion attempt at Cook's Mills in October of 1814. By then the shipbuilding contest on Lake Ontario had been won by Commodore Yeo with the launching of a "super ship," the 102-gun *St. Lawrence*, at Kingston. In October 1814, Brown retreated from Fort Erie to Buffalo, and the Americans finally gave up their invasion of Canada.

### *Artistic Soldiers*

In 1812 British Royal Engineer officers had to be prepared to paint as well as fight. They were trained to sketch and use watercolours because, in the days before photographs, maps and paintings of defences or transportation routes were part of the official reports.

# Living History of 1812

Today you can visit many of the original forts or communities of 1812 and view re-enactments of the battles or participants dressed in authentic uniforms and clothing of those years. Below are some of the places you can visit; contact local tourist offices on both sides of the border for information about exact dates and details.

## Canadian events and forts:
Old Fort York (Toronto, Ontario)
Fort George (Niagara-on-the-Lake, Ontario)
Battle of Stoney Creek (Stoney Creek, Ontario)
Fort Wellington (Prescott, Ontario)
Native and 1812 events (Penetanguishene, Ontario)
Attack on Fort Erie (Fort Erie, Ontario)
Fort Amherstburg (Fort Malden) (Windsor, Ontario)
Nancy Island Historical Site (Wasaga Beach, Ontario)
Backus re-enactors camp (Port Rowan, Ontario)
Old Fort Henry (Kingston, Ontario)
Upper Canada Village (Morrisburg, Ontario)
Heritage Days (Chatham, Ontario)

## American events and forts:
Old Fort Niagara (Youngstown, New York)
Fort Michilimackinac (Mackinac Island, Michigan)
Perry's Flag Ship, U.S. Brig *Niagara* (Erie, Penn.)
Mississinewa (Marion, Indiana)
Fort Snelling (St. Paul, Minnesota)
North West Company Fur Trade Fort (Pine City, Minnesota)
Sackets Harbor Battlefield (Sackets Harbor, New York)
Fort Howard (Green Bay, Wisconsin)
Rendezvous (Prairie du Chien)
Old Fort Madison (Fort Madison, Iowa)
Fort Meigs (Ohio)

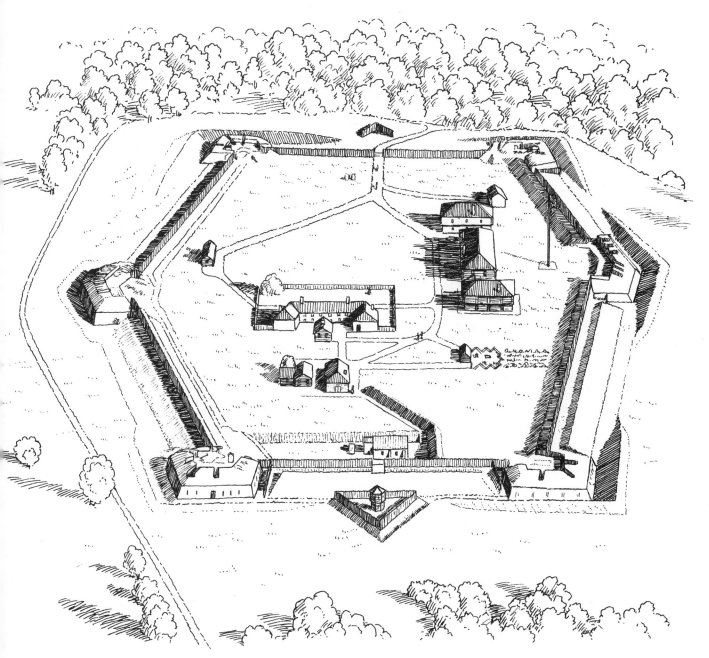

FORT GEORGE, NIAGARA-ON-THE-LAKE, ONTARIO

## 1812 Crossword Puzzle

**ACROSS:**

1. He won the Battle of Lake Erie
3. Nicknamed "Captain Dick"
6. The Peace Treaty
9. A hero at Beaver Dams
11. A doctor and dragoon
12. Nickname for General Dearborn
13. Hero of Upper Canada
14. Canadian-born general
15. Leader of the "Green Tigers" (or "Bloody Boys")
18. Famous lake battle
20. The "One-Armed Captain"
21. Isaac Brock's fiancée
23. Small cannons
28. De Salaberry won this battle
29. He won the Battle of Chippawa
30. Weapon known as "Brown Bess"
31. Half Scottish, Mohawk War Chief
32. He lost the Battle of the Thames

**DOWN:**

2. British commodore on Lake Ontario
4. River where a massacre occurred
5. Original name of Toronto
6. Hero of Stoney Creek
7. Isaak Brock's horse
8. "Flaming-Haired Man"
10. American commodore on Lake Ontario
16. Tecumseh was killed in this battle
17. He burned Prophet's Town
19. General Hull surrendered this fort
22. Leaping Panther
24. Heroine of Upper Canada
25. British general at the Battle of Lake Champlain
26. American general at the Battle of New Orleans
27. First American fort captured in 1812 was on this island

*Answers to 1812 Crossword Puzzle, page 86*

**ACROSS:**
1. Perry
3. Pierpont
6. Ghent
9. Ducharme
11. Chapin
12. Granny
13. Brock
14. Drummond
15. FitzGibbon
18. Erie
20. Barclay
21. Sophie
23. Grasshoppers
28. Châteauguay
29. Scott
30. Musket
31. Norton
32. Proctor

**DOWN:**
2. Yeo
4. Raisin
5. York
6. Green
7. Alfred
8. Dickson
10. Chauncey
16. Thames
17. Harrison
19. Detroit
22. Tecumseh
24. Secord
25. Prevost
26. Jackson
27. Mackinac

## Treaty of Ghent

On December 24, 1814, (Christmas Eve), a peace treaty, overseen by the Czar of Russia, was signed in Ghent, Belgium, between the United States and Britain. The War of 1812 was officially ended. The hard-fighting British, Canadians, and natives had not only beat back every invasion attempt but had captured much American territory. However, the Canadian colonies were represented by British diplomats, far from the frontier, who agreed that both sides would return to their original borders before the war. Fort Michilimackinac, Michigan Territory, Fort Niagara, and other occupied American lands were returned to the United States; Fort Amherstburg and Essex County were returned to Upper Canada. The loyal native tribes who fought with the British and Canadians were not represented, and no guarantee of their land rights was included in the agreement.

## Battle of New Orleans

The destruction and death of war is always a tragedy, but senseless fighting is a travesty. On January 8, 1815, the document signed at Ghent was on its way across the Atlantic Ocean when, unaware that the war was over, a British force of 8000, led by Wellington's brother-in-law, Sir Edward Pakenham, attacked Andrew Jackson's army far to the south near New Orleans. Pakenham and 2000 of his redcoats were killed, and Andrew Jackson later became president of the United States because of his victory at the Battle of New Orleans.

# Index